THE GODS OF PEGANA

LORD DUNSANY

[1905]

PREFACE

In the mists before THE BEGINNING, Fate and Chance cast lots to decide whose the Game should be; and he that won strode through the mists to MANA-YOOD-SUSHAI and said: "Now make gods for Me, for I have won the cast and the Game is to be Mine." Who it was that won the cast, and whether it was Fate or whether Chance that went through the mists before THE BEGINNING to MANA-YOOD-SUSHAI—"none knoweth."

INTRODUCTION

Before there stood gods upon Olympus, or ever Allah was Allah, had wrought and rested MANA-YOOD-SUSHAI.

There are in Pegana Mung and Sish and Kib, and the maker of all small gods, who is MANA-YOOD-SUSHAI. Moreover, we have a faith in Roon and Slid.

And it has been said of old that all things that have been were wrought by the small gods, excepting only MANA-YOOD-SUSHAI, who made the gods and hath thereafter rested.

And none may pray to MANA-YOOD-SUSHAI but only the gods whom he hath made.

But at the Last will MANA-YOOD-SUSHAI forget to rest, and will make again new gods and other worlds, and will destroy the gods whom he hath made.

And the gods and the worlds shall depart, and there shall be only MANA-YOOD-SUSHAI.

OF SKARL THE DRUMMER

When MANA-YOOD-SUSHAI had made the gods and Skarl, Skarl made a drum, and began to beat upon it that he might drum for ever. Then because he was weary after the making of the gods, and because of the drumming of Skarl, did MANA-YOOD-SUSHAI grow drowsy and fall asleep.

And there fell a hush upon the gods when they saw that MANA rested, and there was silence on Pegana save for the drumming of Skarl. Skarl sitteth upon the mist before the feet of MANA-YOOD-SUSHAI, above the gods of Pegana, and there he beateth his drum. Some say that the Worlds and the Suns are but the echoes of the drumming of Skarl, and others say that they be dreams that arise in the mind of MANA because of the drumming of Skarl, as one may dream whose rest is troubled by sound of song, but none knoweth, for who hath heard the voice of MANA-YOOD-SUSHAI, or who hath seen his drummer?

Whether the season be winter or whether it be summer, whether it be morning among the worlds or whether it be night, Skarl still beateth his drum, for the purposes of the gods are not yet fulfilled. Sometimes the arm of Skarl grows weary; but still he beateth his drum, that the gods may do the work of the gods, and the worlds go on, for if he cease for an instant then MANA-YOOD-SUSHAI will start awake, and there will be worlds nor gods no more.

But, when at the last the arm of Skarl shall cease to beat his drum, silence shall startle Pegana like thunder in a cave, and MANA-YOOD-SUSHAI shall cease to rest.

Then shall Skarl put his drum upon his back and walk forth into the void beyond the worlds, because it is THE END, and the work of Skarl is over.

There may arise some other god whom Skarl may serve, or it may be that he shall perish; but to Skarl it shall matter not, for he shall have done the work of Skarl.

OF THE MAKING OF THE WORLDS

When MANA-YOOD-SUSHAI had made the gods there were only the gods, and They sat in the middle of Time, for there was as much Time before them as behind them, which having no end had neither a beginning.

And Pegāna was without heat or light or sound, save for the drumming of Skarl; moreover Pegāna was The Middle of All, for there was below Pegāna what there was above it, and there lay before it that which lay beyond.

Then said the gods, making the signs of the gods and speaking with Their hands lest the silence of Pegāna should blush; then said the gods to one another, speaking with Their hands; "Let Us make worlds to amuse Ourselves while MANA rests. Let Us make worlds and Life and Death, and colours in the sky; only let Us not break the silence upon Pegāna."

Then raising Their hands, each god according to his sign, They made the worlds and the suns, and put a light in the houses of the sky.

Then said the gods: "Let Us make one to seek, to seek and never to find out concerning the wherefore of the making of the gods."

And They made by the lifting of Their hands, each god according to his sign, the Bright One with the flaring tail to seek from the end of the Worlds to the end of them again, to return again after a hundred years.

Man, when thou seest the comet, know that another seeketh besides thee nor ever findeth out.

Then said the gods, still speaking with Their hands: "Let there be now a Watcher to regard."

And They made the Moon, with his face wrinkled with many mountains and worn with a thousand valleys, to regard with pale eyes the games of the small gods, and to watch throughout the resting time of MANA-YOOD-SUSHAI; to watch, to regard all things, and be silent.

Then said the gods: "Let Us make one to rest. One not to move among the moving. One not to seek like the comet, nor to go round like the worlds; to rest while MANA rests."

And They made the Star of the Abiding and set it in the North.

Man, when thou seest the Star of the Abiding to the North, know that one resteth as doth MANA-YOOD-SUSHAI, and know that somewhere among the Worlds is rest.

Lastly the gods said: "We have made worlds and suns, and one to seek and another to regard, let Us now make one to wonder."

And They made Earth to wonder, each god by the uplifting of his hand according to his sign.

And Earth was.

OF THE GAME OF THE GODS

A million years passed over the first game of the gods. And MANA-YOOD-SUSHAI still rested, still in the middle of Time, and the gods still played with Worlds. The Moon regarded, and the Bright One sought, and returned again to his seeking.

Then Kib grew weary of the first game of the gods, and raised his hand in Pegāna, making the sign of Kib, and Earth became covered with beasts for Kib to play with.

And Kib played with beasts.

But the other gods said one to another, speaking with their hands: "What is it that Kib has done?"

And They said to Kib: "What are these things that move upon The Earth yet move not in circles like the Worlds, that regard like the Moon and yet they do not shine?"

And Kib said: "This is Life."

But the gods said one to another: "If Kib has thus made beasts he will in time make Men, and will endanger the Secret of the gods."

And Mung was jealous of the work of Kib, and sent down Death among the beasts, but could not stamp them out.

A million years passed over the second game of the gods, and still it was the Middle of Time.

And Kib grew weary of the second game, and raised his hand in the Middle of All, making the sign of Kib, and made Men: out of beasts he made them, and Earth was covered with Men.

Then the gods feared greatly for the Secret of the gods, and set a veil between Man and his ignorance that he might not understand. And Mung was busy among Men.

But when the other gods saw Kib playing his new game They came and played it too. And this They will play until MANA arises to rebuke Them, saying: "What do ye playing with Worlds and Suns and Men and Life and Death?" And They shall be ashamed of Their playing in the hour of the laughter of MANA-YOOD-SUSHAI.

It was Kib who first broke the Silence of Pegana, by speaking with his mouth like a man.

And all the other gods were angry with Kib that he had spoken with his mouth.

And there was no longer silence in Pegana or the Worlds.

THE CHAUNT OF THE GODS

There came the voice of the gods singing the chaunt of the gods, singing: "We are the gods; We are the little games of MANA-YOOD-SUSHAI that he hath played and hath forgotten.

"MANA-YOOD-SUSHAI hath made us, and We made the Worlds and the Suns.

"And We play with the Worlds and the Sun and Life and Death until MANA arises to rebuke us, saying: 'What do ye playing with Worlds and Suns?'

"It is a very serious thing that there be Worlds and Suns, and yet most withering is the laughter of MANA-YOOD-SUSHAI.

"And when he arises from resting at the Last, and laughs at us for playing with Worlds and Suns, We will hastily put them behind us, and there shall be Worlds no more."

THE SAYINGS OF KIB

(Sender of Life in all the Worlds)

Kib said: "I am Kib. I am none other than Kib."

Kib is Kib. Kib is he and no other. Believe! Kib said: "When Time was early, when Time was very early indeed—there was only MANA-YOOD-SUSHAI. MANA-YOOD-SUSHAI was before the beginning of the gods, and shall be after their going."

And Kib said: "After the going of the gods there will be no small worlds nor big."

Kib said: "It will be lonely for MANA-YOOD-SUSHAI."

Because this is written, believe! For is it not written, or are you greater than Kib? Kib is Kib.

CONCERNING SISH

(The Destroyer of Hours)

Time is the hound of Sish.

At Sish's bidding do the hours run before him as he goeth upon his way.

Never hath Sish stepped backward nor ever hath he tarried; never hath he relented to the things that once he knew nor turned to them again.

Before Sish is Kib, and behind him goeth Mung.

Very pleasant are all things before the face of Sish, but behind him they are withered and old.

And Sish goeth ceaselessly upon his way.

Once the gods walked upon Earth as men walk and spake with their mouths like Men. That was in Wornath-Mavai. They walk not now.

And Wornath-Mavai was a garden fairer than all the gardens upon Earth.

Kib was propitious, and Mung raised not his hand against it, neither did Sish assail it with his hours.

Wornath-Mavai lieth in a valley and looketh towards the south, and on the slopes of it Sish rested among the flowers when Sish was young.

Thence Sish went forth into the world to destroy its cities, and to provoke his hours to assail all things, and to batter against them with the rust and with the dust.

And Time, which is the hound of Sish, devoured all things; and Sish sent up the ivy and fostered weeds, and dust fell from the hand of Sish and covered stately things. Only the valley where Sish rested when he and Time were young did Sish not provoke his hours to assail.

There he restrained his old hound Time, and at its borders Mung withheld his footsteps.

Wornath-Mavai still lieth looking towards the south, a garden among gardens, and still the flowers grow about its slopes as they grew when the gods were young; and even the butterflies live in Wornath-Mavai still. For the minds of the gods relent towards their earliest memories, who relent not otherwise at all.

Wornath-Mavai still lieth looking towards the south; but if thou shouldst ever find it thou art then more fortunate than the gods, because they walk not in Wornath-Mavai now.

Once did the prophet think that he discerned it in the distance beyond mountains, a garden exceeding fair with flowers; but Sish arose, and pointed with his hand, and set his hound to pursue him, who hath followed ever since.

Time is the hound of the gods; but it hath been said of old that he will one day turn upon his masters, and seek to slay the gods, excepting only MANA-YOOD-SUSHAI, whose dreams are the gods themselves—dreamed long ago.

THE SAYINGS OF SLID

(Whose Soul is by the Sea)

Slid said: "Let no man pray to MANA-YOOD-SUSHAI, for who shall trouble MANA with mortal woes or irk him with the sorrows of all the houses of Earth?

"Nor let any sacrifice to MANA-YOOD-SUSHAI, for what glory shall he find in sacrifices or altars who hath made the gods themselves?

"Pray to the small gods, who are the gods of Doing; but MANA is the god of Having Done—the god of Having Done and of the Resting.

"Pray to the small gods and hope that they may hear thee. Yet what mercy should the small gods have, who themselves made Death and Pain; or shall they restrain their old hound Time for thee?

"Slid is but a small god. Yet Slid is Slid—it is written and hath been said. "Pray, thou, therefore, to Slid, and forget not Slid, and it may be that Slid will not forget to send thee Death when most thou needest it."

And the People of Earth said: "There is a melody upon the Earth as though ten thousand streams all sang together for their homes that they had forsaken in the hills."

And Slid said: "I am the Lord of gliding waters and of foaming waters and of still. I am the Lord of all the waters in the world and all that long streams garner in the hills; but the soul of Slid is in the Sea. Thither goes all that glides upon Earth, and the end of all the rivers is the Sea."

And Slid said: "The hand of Slid hath toyed with cataracts, and down the valleys have trod the feet of Slid, and out of the lakes of the plains regard the eyes of Slid; but the soul of Slid is in the sea."

Much homage hath Slid among the cities of men and pleasant are the woodland paths and the paths of the plains, and pleasant the high valleys where he danceth in the hills; but Slid would be fettered neither by banks nor boundaries—so the soul of Slid is in the Sea.

For there may Slid repose beneath the sun and smile at the gods above him with all the smiles of Slid, and be a happier god than Those who sway the Worlds, whose work is Life and Death.

There may he sit and smile, or creep among the ships, or moan and sigh round islands in his great content—the miser lord of wealth in gems and pearls beyond the telling of all fables.

Or there may he, when Slid would fain exult, throw up his great arms, or toss with many a fathom of wandering hair the mighty head of Slid, and cry aloud tumultuous dirges of shipwreck, and feel through all his being the crashing might of Slid, and sway the sea. Then doth the Sea, like venturous legions on the eve of war that exult to acclaim their chief, gather its force together from under all the winds and roar and follow and sing and crash together to vanquish all things—and all at the bidding of Slid, whose soul is in the sea.

There is ease in the soul of Slid and there be calms upon the sea; also, there be storms upon the sea and troubles in the soul of Slid, for the gods have many moods. And Slid is in many places, for he sitteth in high Pegana. Also along the valleys walketh Slid, wherever water moveth or lieth still; but the voice and the cry of Slid are from the sea. And to whoever that cry hath ever come he must needs follow and follow, leaving all stable things; only to be always with Slid in all the moods of Slid, to find no rest until he reaches the sea.

With the cry of Slid before them and the hills of their home behind have gone a hundred thousand to the sea, over whose bones doth Slid lament with the voice of a god lamenting for his people. Even the streams from the inner lands have heard Slid's far-off cry, and all together have forsaken lawns and trees to follow where Slid is gathering up his own, to rejoice where Slid rejoices, singing the chaunt of Slid, even as will at the Last gather all the Lives of the People about the feet of MANA-YOOD-SUSHAI.

THE DEEDS OF MUNG

(Lord of all Deaths between Pegana and the Rim)

Once, as Mung went his way athwart the Earth and up and down its cities and across its plains, Mung came upon a man who was afraid when Mung said: "I am Mung!"

And Mung said: "Were the forty million years before thy coming intolerable to thee?"

And Mung said: "Not less tolerable to thee shall be the forty million years to come!"

Then Mung made against him the sign of Mung and the Life of the Man was fettered no longer with hands and feet.

At the end of the flight of the arrow there is Mung, and in the houses and the cities of Men. Mung walketh in all places at all times. But mostly he loves to walk in the dark and still, along the river mists when the wind hath sank, a little before night meeteth with the morning upon the highway between Pegana and the Worlds.

Sometimes Mung entereth the poor man's cottage; Mung also boweth very low before The King. Then do the Lives of the poor man and of The King go forth among the Worlds.

And Mung said: "Many turnings hath the road that Kib hath given every man to tread upon the earth. Behind one of these turnings sitteth Mung."

One day as a man trod upon the road that Kib had given him to tread he came suddenly upon Mung. And when Mung said: "I am Mung!" the man cried out: "Alas, that I took this road, for had I gone by any other way then had I not met with Mung."

And Mung said: "Had it been possible for thee to go by any other way then had the Scheme of Things been otherwise and the gods had been other gods. When MANA-YOOD-SUSHAI forgets to rest and makes again new gods it may be that They will send thee again into the Worlds; and then thou mayest choose some other way, and not meet with Mung."

Then Mung made the sign of Mung. And the Life of that man went forth with yesterday's regrets and all old sorrows and forgotten things—whither Mung knoweth.

And Mung went onward with his work to sunder Life from flesh, and Mung came upon a man who became stricken with sorrow when he saw the shadow of Mung. But Mung said: "When at the sign of Mung thy Life shall float away there will also disappear thy sorrow at forsaking it." But the man cried out: "O Mung! tarry for a little, and make not the sign of Mung against me now, for I have a family upon the earth with whom sorrow will remain, though mine should disappear because of the sign of Mung."

And Mung said: "With the gods it is always Now. And before Sish hath banished many of the years the sorrows of thy family for thee shall go the way of thine." And the man beheld Mung making the sign of Mung before his eyes, which beheld things no more.

THE CHAUNT OF THE PRIESTS

This is the chaunt of the Priests.

The chaunt of the priests of Mung.

This is the chaunt of the Priests.

All day long to Mung cry out the Priests of Mung, and, yet Mung harkeneth not. What, then, shall avail the prayers of All the People?

Rather bring gifts to the Priests, gifts to the Priests of Mung.

So shall they cry louder unto Mung than ever was their wont.

And it may be that Mung shall hear.

Not any longer than shall fall the Shadow of Mung athwart the hopes of the People.

Not any longer then shall the Tread of Mung darken the dreams of the people.

Not any longer shall the lives of the People be loosened because of Mung.

Bring ye gifts to the Priests, gifts to the Priests of Mung.

This is the chaunt of the Priests.

The chaunt of the Priests of Mung.

This is the chaunt of the Priests.

THE SAYINGS OF LIMPANG-TUNG

(The God of Mirth and of Melodious Minstrels)

And Limpang-Tung said: "The ways of the gods are strange. The flower groweth up and the flower fadeth away. This may be very clever of the gods. Man groweth from his infancy, and in a while he dieth. This may be very clever too.

"But the gods play with a strange scheme.

"I will send jests into the world and a little mirth. And while Death seems to thee as far away as the purple rim of hills; or sorrow as far off as rain in the blue days of summer, then pray to Limpang-Tung. But when thou growest old, or ere thou diest, pray not of Limpang-Tung, for thou becomest part of a scheme that he doth not understand.

"Go out into the starry night, and Limpang-Tung will dance with thee who danced since the gods were young, the god of mirth and of melodious minstrels. Or offer up a jest to Limpang-Tung; only pray not in thy sorrow to Limpang-Tung, for he saith of sorrow: 'It may be very clever of the gods,' but he doth not understand."

And Limpang-Tung said: "I am lesser than the gods; pray, therefore, to the small gods and not to Limpang-Tung.

"Natheless between Pegana and the Earth flutter ten thousand thousand prayers that beat their wings against the face of Death, and never for one of them hath the hand of the Striker been stayed, nor yet have tarried the feet of the Relentless One.

"Utter thy prayer! It may accomplish where failed ten thousand thousand.

"Limpang-Tung is lesser than the gods, and doth not understand."

And Limpang-Tung said: "Lest men grow weary down on the great Worlds through gazing always at a changeless sky, I will paint my pictures in the sky. And I will paint them twice in every day for so long as days shall be. Once as the day ariseth out of the homes of dawn will I paint the Blue, that men may see and rejoice; and ere day falleth under into the night will I paint upon the Blue again, lest men be sad.

"It is a little," said Limpang-Tung, "it is a little even for a god to give some pleasure to men upon the Worlds."

And Limpang-Tung hath sworn that the pictures that he paints shall never be the same for so long as the days shall be, and this he hath sworn by the oath of the gods of Pegana that the gods may never break, laying his hand upon the shoulder of each of the gods and swearing by the light behind Their eyes.

Limpang-Tung hath lured a melody out of the stream and stolen its anthem from the forest; for him the wind hath cried in lonely places and the ocean sung its dirges. There is music for Limpang-Tung in the sounds of the moving of grass and in the voices of the people that lament or in the cry of them that rejoice.

In an inner mountain land where none hath come he hath carved his organ pipes out of the mountains, and there when the winds, his servants, come in from all the world he maketh the melody of Limpang-Tung. But the song, arising at night, goeth forth like a river, winding through all the world, and here and there amid the peoples of earth one heareth, and straightaway all that hath voice to sing crieth aloud in music to his soul.

Or sometimes walking through the dusk with steps unheard by men, in a form unseen by the people, Limpang-Tung goeth abroad, and, standing behind the minstrels in cities of song, waveth his hands above them to and fro, and the minstrels bend to their work, and the voice of the music ariseth; and mirth and melody abound in that city of song, and no one seeth Limpang-Tung as he standeth behind the minstrels.

But through the mists towards morning, in the dark when the minstrels sleep and mirth and melody have sunk to rest, Limpang-Tung goeth back again to his mountain land.

OF YOHARNETH-LAHAI

(The God of Little Dreams and Fancies)

Yaoharneth-Lahai is the god of little dreams and fancies.

All night he sendeth little dreams out of Pegana to please the people of Earth.

He sendeth little dreams to the poor man and to The King.

He is so busy to send his dreams to all before the night be ended that oft he forgetteth which be the poor man and which be The King.

To whom Yoharneth-Lahai cometh not with little dreams and sleep he must endure all night the laughter of the gods, with highest mockery, in Pegana.

All night long Yoharneth-Lahai giveth peace to cities until the dawn hour and the departing of Yoharneth-Lahai, when it is time for the gods to play with men again.

Whether the dreams and the fancies of Yoharneth-Lahai be false and the Things that are done in the Day be real, or the Things that are done in the Day be false and the dreams and the fancies of Yoharneth-Lahai be true, none knoweth saving only MANA-YOOD-SUSHAI, who hath not spoken.

OF ROON, THE GOD OF GOING, AND THE THOUSAND HOME GODS

Roon said: "There be gods of moving and gods of standing still, but I am the god of Going."

It is because of Roon that the worlds are never still, for the moons and the worlds and the comet are stirred by the spirit of Roon, which saith: "Go! Go! Go!"

Roon met the Worlds all in the morning of Things, before there was light upon Pegana, and Roon danced before them in the Void, since when they are never still, Roon sendeth all streams to the Sea, and all the rivers to the soul of Slid.

Roon maketh the sign of Roon before the waters, and lo! they have left the hills; and Roon hath spoken in the ear of the North Wind that he may be still no more.

The footfall of Roon hath been heard at evening outside the houses of men, and thenceforth comfort and abiding know them no more. Before them stretcheth travel over all the lands, long miles, and never resting between their homes and their graves—and all at the bidding of Roon.

The Mountains have set no limit against Roon nor all the seas a boundary.

Whither Roon hath desired there must Roon's people go, and the worlds and their streams and the winds.

I heard the whisper of Roon at evening, saying: "There are islands of spices to the South," and the voice of Roon saying: "Go."

And Roon said: "There are a thousand home gods, the little gods that sit before the hearth and mind the fire—there is one Roon."

Roon saith in a whisper, in a whisper when none heareth, when the sun is low: "What doeth MANA-YOOD-SUSHAI?" Roon is no god that thou mayest worship by thy hearth, nor will he be benignant to thy home.

Offer to Roon thy toiling and thy speed, whose incense is the smoke of the camp fire to the South, whose song is the sound of going, whose temples stand beyond the farthest hills in his lands behind the East.

Yarinareth, Yarinareth, Yarinareth, which signifieth Beyond—these words be carved in letters of gold upon the arch of the great portal of the Temple of Roon that men have builded looking towards the East upon the Sea, where Roon is carved as a giant trumpeter, with his trumpet pointing towards the East beyond the Seas.

Whoso heareth his voice, the voice of Roon at evening, he at once forsaketh the home gods that sit beside the hearth. These be the gods of the hearth: Pitsu, who stroketh the cat; Hobith who calms the dog; and Habaniah, the lord of glowing embers; and little Zumbiboo, the lord of dust; and old Gribaun, who sits in the heart of the fire to turn the wood to ash—all these be home gods, and live not in Pegana and be lesser than Roon

There is also Kilooloogung, the lord of arising smoke, who taketh the smoke from the hearth and sendeth it to the sky, who is pleased if it reacheth Pegana, so that the gods of Pegana, speaking to the gods, say: "There is Kilooloogung doing the work on earth of Kilooloogung."

All these are gods so small that they be lesser than men, but pleasant gods to have beside the hearth; and often men have prayed to Kilooloogung, saying: "Thou whose smoke ascendeth to Pegāna send up with it our prayers, that the gods may hear." And Kilooloogung, who is pleased that men should pray, stretches himself up all grey and lean, with his arms above his head, and sendeth his servant the smoke to seek Pegāna, that the gods of Pegāna may know that the people pray.

And Jabim is the Lord of broken things, who sitteth behind the house to lament the things that are cast away. And there he sitteth lamenting the broken things until the worlds be ended, or until someone cometh to mend the broken things. Or sometimes he sitteth by the river's edge to lament the forgotten things that drift upon it.

A kindly god is Jabim, whose heart is sore if anything be lost.

There is also Triboogie, the Lord of Dusk, whose children are the shadows, who sitteth in a corner far off from Habaniah and speaketh to none. But after Habaniah hath gone to sleep and old Gribaun hath blinked a hundred times, until he forgetteth which be wood or ash, then doth Triboogie send his children to run about the room and dance upon the walls, but never disturb the silence.

But when there is light again upon the worlds, and dawn comes dancing down the highway from Pegāna, then does Triboogie retire into his corner, with his children all around him, as though they had never danced about the room. And the slaves of Habaniah and old Gribaun come and awake them from their sleep upon the hearth, and Pitsu strokes the cat, and Hobith calms the dog, and Kilooloogung stretches aloft his arms towards Pegana, and Triboogie is very still, and his children asleep.

And when it is dark, all in the hour of Triboogie, Hish creepeth from the forest, the Lord of Silence, whose children are the bats, that have broken the command of their father, but in a voice that is ever so low. Hish husheth the mouse and all the whispers in the night; he maketh all noises still. Only the cricket rebelleth. But Hish hath set against him such a spell that after he hath cried a thousand times his voice may be heard no more but becometh part of the silence.

And when he hath slain all sounds Hish boweth low to the ground; then cometh into the house, with never a sound of feet, the god Yoharneth-Lahai.

But away in the forest whence Hish hath come Wohoon, the Lord of Noises in the Night, awaketh in his lair and creepeth round the forest to see whether it be true that Hish hath gone.

Then in some glade Wohoon lifts up his voice and cries aloud, that all the night may hear, that it is he, Wohoon, who is abroad in all the forest. And the wolf and the fox and the owl, and the great beasts and the small, lift up their voices to acclaim Wohoon. And there arise the sounds of voices and the stirring of leaves.

THE REVOLT OF THE HOME GODS

There be three broad rivers of the plain, born before memory or fable, whose mothers are three grey peaks and whose father was the storm. There names be Eimës, Zänës, and Segástrion.

And Eimës is the joy of lowing herds; and Zänës hath bowed his neck to the yoke of man, and carries the timber from the forest far up below the mountain; and Segástrion sings old songs to shepherd boys, singing of his childhood in a lone ravine and of how he once sprang down the mountain sides and far away into the plain to see the world, and of how one day at last he will find the sea. These be the rivers of the plain, wherein the plain rejoices. But old men tell, whose fathers heard it from the ancients, how once the lords of the three rivers of the plain rebelled against the law of the Worlds, and passed beyond their boundaries, and joined together and whelmed cities and slew men, saying: "We now play the game of the gods and slay men for our pleasure, and we be greater than the gods of Pegana."

And all the plain was flooded to the hills.

And Eimës, Zänës, and Segástrion sat upon the mountains, and spread their hands over their rivers that rebelled by their command.

But the prayer of men going upward found Pegana, and cried in the ear of the gods: "There be three home gods who slay us for their pleasure, and say that they be mightier than Pegana's gods, and play Their game with men."

Then were all the gods of Pegana very wroth; but They could not whelm the lords of the three rivers, because being home gods, though small, they were immortal.

And still the home gods spread their hands across their rivers, with their fingers wide apart, and the waters rose and rose, and the voice of their torrent grew louder, crying: "Are we not Eimës, Zänës, and Segástrion?"

Then Mung went down into a waste of Afrik, and came upon the drought Umbool as he sat in the desert upon iron rocks, clawing with miserly grasp at the bones of men and breathing hot.

And Mung stood before him as his dry sides heaved, and ever as they sank his hot breath blasted dry sticks and bones.

Then Mung said: "Friend of Mung! Go, thou and grin before the faces of Eimës, Zänës, and Segástrion till they see whether it be wise to rebel against the gods of Pegāna."

And Umbool answered: "I am the beast of Mung."

And Umbool came and crouched upon a hill upon the other side of the waters and grinned across them at the rebellious home gods.

And whenever Eimës, Zänës, and Segástrion stretched out their hands over their rivers they saw before their faces the grinning of Umbool; and because the grinning was like death in a hot and hideous land therefore they turned away and spread their hands no more over their rivers, and the waters sank and sank.

But when Umbool had grinned for thirty days the waters fell back into the river beds and the lords of the rivers slunk away back again to their homes: still Umbool sat and grinned.

Then Eimës sought to hide himself in a great pool beneath a rock, and Zänës crept into the middle of a wood, and Segástrion lay and panted on the sand—still Umbool sat and grinned.

And Eimës grew lean, and was forgotten, so that the men of the plain would say: "Here once was Eimës"; and Zänës scarce had strength to lead his river to the sea; and as Segástrion lay and panted a man stepped over his stream, and Segástrion said: "It is the foot of a man that has passed across my neck, and I have sought to be greater than the gods of Pegāna."

Then said the gods of Pegāna: "It is enough. We are the gods of Pegāna, and none are equal."

Then Mung sent Umbool back to his waste in Afrik to breathe again upon the rocks, and parch the desert, and to sear the memory of Afrik into the brains of all who ever bring their bones away.

And Eimës, Zänës, and Segástrion sang again, and walked once more in their accustomed haunts, and played the game of Life and Death with fishes and frogs, but never essayed to play it any more with men, as do the gods of Pegāna.

OF DOROZHAND

(Whose Eyes Regard The End)

Sitting above the lives of the people, and looking, doth Dorozhand see that which is to be.

The god of Destiny is Dorozhand. Upon whom have looked the eyes of Dorozhand he goeth forward to an end that naught may stay; he becometh the arrow from the bow of Dorozhand hurled forward at a mark he may not see—to the goal of Dorozhand. Beyond the thinking of men, beyond the sight of all the other gods, regard the eyes of Dorozhand.

He hath chosen his slaves. And them doth the destiny god drive onward where he will, who, knowing not whither nor even knowing why, feel only his scourge behind them or hear his cry before.

There is something that Dorozhand would fain achieve, and, therefore, hath he set the people striving, with none to cease or rest in all the worlds. But the gods of Pegana, speaking to the gods, say: "What is it that Dorozhand would fain achieve?"

It hath been written and said that not only the destinies of men are the care of Dorozhand but that even the gods of Pegana be not unconcerned by his will.

All the gods of Pegana have felt a fear, for they have seen a look in the eyes of Dorozhand that regardeth beyond the gods.

The reason and purpose of the Worlds is that there should be Life upon the Worlds, and Life is the instrument of Dorozhand wherewith he would achieve his end.

Therefore the Worlds go on, and the rivers run to the sea, and Life ariseth and flieth even in all the Worlds, and the gods of Pegana do the work of the gods—and all for Dorozhand. But when the end of Dorozhand hath been achieved there will be need no longer of Life upon the Worlds, nor any more a game for the small gods to play. Then will Kib tiptoe gently across Pegana to the resting-place in Highest Pegana of MANA-YOOD-SUSHAI, and touching reverently his hand, the hand that wrought the gods, say: "MANA-YOOD-SUSHAI, thou hast rested long."

And MANA-YOOD-SUSHAI shall say: "Not so; for I have rested for but fifty aeons of the gods, each of them scarce more than ten million mortal years of the Worlds that ye have made."

And then shall the gods be afraid when they find that MANA knoweth that they have made Worlds while he rested. And they shall answer: "Nay; but the Worlds came all of themselves."

Then MANA-YOOD-SUSHAI, as one who would have done with an irksome matter, will lightly wave his hand—the hand that wrought the gods—and there shall be gods no more.

When there shall be three moons towards the north above the Star of the Abiding, three moons that neither wax nor wane but regard towards the North.

Or when the comet ceaseth from his seeking and stands still, not any longer moving among the Worlds but tarrying as one who rests after the end of search, then shall arise from resting, because it is THE END, the Greater One, who rested of old time, even MANA-YOOD-SUSHAI.

Then shall the Times that were be Times no more; and it may be that the old, dead days shall return from beyond the Rim, and we who have wept for them shall see those days again, as one who, returning from long travel to his home, comes suddenly on dear, remembered things.

For none shall know of MANA who hath rested for so long, whether he be a harsh or merciful god. It may be that he shall have mercy, and that these things shall be.

THE EYE IN THE WASTE

There lie seven deserts beyond Bodrahan, which is the city of the caravans' end. None goeth beyond. In the first desert lie the tracks of mighty travellers outward from Bodrahan, and some returning. And in the second lie only outward tracks, and none return.

The third is a desert untrodden by the feet of men.

The fourth is the desert of sand, and the fifth is the desert of dust, and the sixth is the desert of stones, and the seventh is the Desert of Deserts.

In the midst of the last of the deserts that lie beyond Bodrahan, in the centre of the Desert of Deserts, standeth the image that hath been hewn of old out of the living hill whose name is Ranorada—the eye in the waste.

About the base of Ranorada is carved in mystic letters that are vaster than the beds of streams these words:

To the god who knows.

Now, beyond the second desert are no tracks, and there is no water in all the seven deserts that lie beyond Bodrahan. Therefore came no man thither to hew that statue from the living hills, and Ranorada was wrought by the hands of gods. Men tell in Bodrahan, where the caravans end and all the drivers of the camels rest, how once the gods hewed Ranorada from the living hill, hammering all night long beyond the deserts. Moreover, they say that Ranorada is carved in the likeness of the god Hoodrazai, who hath found the secret of MANA-YOOD-SUSHAI, and knoweth the wherefore of the making of the gods.

They say that Hoodrazai stands all alone in Pegāna and speaks to none because he knows what is hidden from the gods.

Therefore the gods have made his image in a lonely land as one who thinks and is silent—the eye in the waste.

They say that Hoodrazai had heard the murmers of MANA-YOOD-SUSHAI as he muttered to himself, and gleaned the meaning, and knew; and that he was the god of mirth and of abundant joy, but became from the moment of his knowing a mirthless god, even as his image, which regards the deserts beyond the track of man.

But the camel drivers, as they sit and listen to the tales of the old men in the market-place of Bodrahan, at evening, while the camels rest, say:

"If Hoodrazai is so very wise and yet is sad, let us drink wine, and banish wisdom to the wastes that lie beyond Bodrahan." Therefore is there feasting and laughter all night long in the city where the caravans end.

All this the camel drivers tell when the caravans come in from Bodrahan; but who shall credit tales that camel drivers have heard from aged men in so remote a city?

OF THE THING THAT IS NEITHER GOD NOR BEAST

Seeing that wisdom is not in cities nor happiness in wisdom, and because Yadin the prophet was doomed by the gods ere he was born to go in search of wisdom, he followed the caravans to Bodrahan. There in the evening, where the camels rest, when the wind of the day ebbs out into the desert sighing amid the palms its last farewells and leaving the caravans still, he sent his prayer with the wind to drift into the desert calling to Hoodrazai.

And down the wind his prayer went calling: "Why do the gods endure, and play their game with men? Why doth not Skarl forsake his drumming, and MANA cease to rest?" and the echo of seven deserts answered: "Who knows? Who knows?"

But out in the waste, beyond the seven deserts where Ranorada looms enormous in the dusk, at evening his prayer was heard; and from the rim of the waste whither had gone his prayer, came three flamingoes flying, and their voices said: "Going South, Going South" at every stroke of their wings.

But as they passed by the prophet they seemed so cool and free and the desert so blinding and hot that he stretched up his arms towards them. Then it seemed happy to fly and pleasant to follow behind great white wings, and he was with the three flamingoes up in the cool above the desert, and their voices cried before him: "Going South, Going South," and the desert below him mumbled: "Who knows? Who knows?"

Sometimes the earth stretched up towards them with peaks of mountains, sometimes it fell away in steep ravines, blue rivers sang to them as they passed above them, or very faintly came the song of breezes in lone orchards, and far away the sea sang mighty dirges of old forsaken isles. But it seemed that in all the world there was nothing only to be going South.

It seemed that somewhere the South was calling to her own, and that they were going South.

But when the prophet saw that they had passed above the edge of Earth, and that far away to the North of them lay the Moon, he perceived that he was following no mortal birds but some strange messengers of Hoodrazai whose nest had lain in one of Pegana's vales below the mountains whereon sit the gods.

Still they went South, passing by all the Worlds and leaving them to the North, till only Araxes, Zadres, and Hyraglion lay still to the South of them, where great Ingazi seemed only a point of light, and Yo and Mindo could be seen no more.

Still they went South till they passed below the South and came to the Rim of the Worlds.

There there is neither South nor East nor West, but only North and Beyond; there is only North of it where lie the Worlds, and Beyond it where lies the Silence, and the Rim is a mass of rocks that were never used by the gods when They made the Worlds, and on it sat Trogool. Trogool is the Thing that is neither god nor beast, who neither howls nor breathes, only *It* turns over the leaves of a great book, black and white, black and white for ever until THE END.

And all that is to be is written in the book is also all that was.

When *It* turneth a black page it is night, and when *It* turneth a white page it is day.

Because it is written that there are gods—there are the gods.

Also there is writing about thee and me until the page where our names no more are written.

Then as the prophet watched *It*, Trogool turned a page—a black one, and night was over, and day shone on the Worlds.

Trogool is the Thing that men in many countries have called by many names. *It* is the Thing that sits behind the gods, whose book is the Scheme of Things.

But when Yadin saw that old remembered days were hidden away with the part that *It* had turned, and knew that upon one whose name is writ no more the last page had turned for ever a thousand pages back. Then did he utter his prayer in the fact of Trogool who only turns the pages and never answers prayer. He prayed in the face of Trogool: "Only turn back thy pages to the name of one which is writ no more, and far away upon a place named Earth shall rise the prayers of a little people that acclaim the name of Trogool, for there is indeed far off a place called Earth where men shall pray to Trogool."

Then spake Trogool who turns the pages and never answers prayer, and his voice was like the murmurs of the waste at night when echoes have been lost: "Though the whirlwind of the South should tug with his claws at a page that hath been turned yet shall he not be able to ever turn it back."

Then because of words in the book that said that it should be so, Yadin found himself lying in the desert where one gave him water, and afterwards carried him on a camel into Bodrahan.

There some said that he had but dreamed when thirst seized him while he wandered among the rocks in the desert. But certain aged men of Bodrahan say that indeed there sitteth somewhere a Thing that is called Trogool, that is neither god nor beast, that turneth the leaves of a book, black and white, black and white, until he come to the words: *Mai Doon Izahn*, which means The End For Ever, and book and gods and worlds shall be no more.

YONATH THE PROPHET

Yonath was the first among prophets who uttered unto men.

These are the words of Yonath, the first among all prophets:

There be gods upon Pegāna.

Upon a night I slept. And in my sleep Pegāna came very near. And Pegāna was full of gods.

I saw the gods beside me as one might see wonted things.

Only I saw not MANA-YOOD-SUSHAI.

And in that hour, in the hour of my sleep, I knew.

And the end and the beginning of my knowing, and all of my knowing that there was, was this—that Man Knoweth Not.

Seek thou to find at night the utter edge of the darkness, or seek to find the birthplace of the rainbow where he leapeth upward from the hills, only seek not concerning the wherefore of the making of the gods.

The gods have set a brightness upon the farther side of the Things to Come that they may appear more felititous to men than the Things that Are.

To the gods the Things to Come are but as the Things that Are, and nothing altereth in Pegāna.

The gods, although not merciful, are not ferocious gods. They are the destroyers of the Days that Were, but they set a glory about the Days to Be.

Man must endure the Days that Are, but the gods have left him his ignorance as a solace.

Seek not to know. Thy seeking will weary thee, and thou wilt return much worn, to rest at last about the place from whence thou settest out upon thy seeking.

Seek not to know. Even I, Yonath, the oldest prophet, burdened with the wisdom of great years, and worn with seeking, know only that man knoweth not.

Once I set out seeking to know all things. Now I know one thing only, and soon the Years will carry me away.

The path of my seeking, that leadeth to seeking again, must be trodden by very many more, when Yonath is no longer even Yonath.

Set not thy foot upon that path.

Seek not to know.

These be the Words of Yonath.

YUG THE PROPHET

When the Years had carries away Yonath, and Yonath was dead, there was no longer a prophet among men.

And still men sought to know.

Therefore they said unto Yug: "Be thou our prophet, and know all things, and tell us concerning the wherefore of It All."

And Yug said: "I know all things." And men were pleased.

And Yug said of the Beginning that it was in Yug's own garden, and of the End that it was in the sight of Yug.

And men forgot Yug.

One day Yug saw Mung behind the hills making the sign of Mung. And Yug was Yug no more.

ALHIRETH-HOTEP THE PROPHET

When Yug was Yug no more men said unto Alhireth-Hotep: "Be thou our prophet, and be as wise as Yug."

And Alhireth-Hotep said: "I am as wise as Yug." And men were very glad.

And Alhireth-Hotep said of Life and Death: "These be the affairs of Alhireth-Hotep." And men brought gifts to him.

One day Alhireth-Hotep wrote in a book: "Alhireth-Hotep knoweth All Things, for he hath spoken with Mung."

And Mung stepped from behind him, making the sign of Mung, saying: "Knowest thou All Things, then, Alhireth-Hotep?" And Alhireth-Hotep became among the Things that Were.

KABOK THE PROPHET

When Alhireth-Hotep was among the Things that Were, and still men sought to know, they said unto Kabok: "Be thou as wise as was Alhireth-Hotep."

And Kabok grew wise in his own sight and in the sight of men.

And Kabok said: "Mung maketh his signs against men or withholdeth it by the advice of Kabok."

And he said unto one: "Thou hast sinned against Kabok, therefore will Mung make the sign of Mung against thee." And to another: "Thou has brought Kabok gifts, therefore shall Mung forbear to make against thee the sign of Mung."

One night as Kabok fattened upon the gifts that men had brought him he heard the tread of Mung treading in the garden of Kabok about his house at night.

And because the night was very still it seemed most evil to Kabok that Mung should be treading in his garden, without the advice of Kabok, about his house at night.

And Kabok, who knew All Things, grew afraid, for the treading was very loud and the night still, and he knew not what lay behind the back of Mung, which none had ever seen.

But when the morning grew to brightness, and there was light upon the Worlds, and Mung trod no longer in the garden, Kabok forgot his fears, and said: "Perhaps it was but a herd of cattle that stampeded in the garden of Kabok."

And Kabok went about his business, which was that of knowing All Things, and telling All Things unto men, and making light of Mung.

But that night Mung trod again in the garden of Kabok, about his house at night, and stood before the window of the house like a shadow standing erect, so that Kabok knew indeed that it was Mung.

And a great fear fell upon the throat of Kabok, so that his speech was hoarse; and he cried out: "Thou art Mung!"

And Mung slightly inclined his head, and went on to tread in the garden of Kabok, about his house at night.

And Kabok lay and listened with horror at his heart.

But when the second morning grew to brightness, and there was light upon the Worlds, Mung went from treading in the garden of Kabok; and for a little while Kabok hoped, but looked with great dread for the coming of the third night.

And when the third night was come, and the bat had gone to his home, and the wind had sank, the night was very still.

And Kabok lay and listened, to whom the wings of the night flew very slow.

But, ere night met the morning upon the highway between Pegana and the Worlds, there came the tread of Mung in the garden of Kabok towards Kabok's door.

And Kabok fled out of his house as flees a hunted beast and flung himself before Mung.

And Mung made the sign of Mung, pointing towards THE END.

And the fears of Kabok had rest from troubling Kabok any more, for they and he were among accomplished things.

OF THE CALAMITY THAT BEFEL YUN-ILARA BY THE SEA, AND OF THE BUILDING OF THE TOWER OF THE ENDING OF DAYS

When Kabok and his fears had rest the people sought a prophet who should have no fear of Mung, whose hand was against the prophets.

And at last they found Yun-Ilara, who tended sheep and had no fear of Mung, and the people brought him to the town that he might be their prophet.

And Yun-Ilara builded a tower towards the sea that looked upon the setting of the Sun. And he called it the Tower of the Ending of Days.

And about the ending of the day would Yun-Ilara go up to his tower's top and look towards the setting of the Sun to cry his curses against Mung, crying: "O Mung! whose hand is against the Sun, whom men abhor but worship because they fear thee, here stands and speaks a man who fears thee not. Assassin lord of murder and dark things, abhorrent, merciless, make thou the sign of Mung against me when thou wilt, but until silence settles upon my lips, because of the sign of Mung, I will curse Mung to his face." And the people in the street below would gaze up with wonder towards Yun-Ilara, who had no fear of Mung, and brought him gifts; only in their homes after the falling of the night would they pray again with reverence to Mung. But Mung said: "Shall a man curse a god?"

And still Mung came not nigh to Yun-Ilara as he cried his curses against Mung from his tower towards the sea.

And Sish throughout the Worlds hurled Time away, and slew the Hours that had served him well, and called up more out of the timeless waste that lieth beyond the Worlds, and drave them forth to assail all things. And Sish cast a whiteness over the hairs of Yun-Ilara, and ivy about his tower, and weariness over his limbs, for Mung passed by him still.

And when Sish became a god less durable to Yun-Ilara than ever Mung hath been he ceased at last to cry from his tower's top his curses against Mung whenever the sun went down, till there came the day when weariness of the gift of Kib fell heavily upon Yun-Ilara.

Then from the tower of the Ending of Days did Yun-Ilara cry out thus to Mung, crying: "O Mung! O loveliest of the gods! O Mung, most dearly to be desired! thy gift of Death is the heritage of Man, with ease and rest and silence and returning to the Earth. Kib giveth but toil and trouble; and Sish, he sendeth regrets with each of his hours wherewith he assails the World. Yoharneth-Lahai cometh nigh no more. I can no longer be glad with Limpang-Tung. When the other gods forsake him a man hath only Mung."

But Mung said: "Shall a man curse a god?"

And every day and all night long did Yun-Ilara cry aloud: "Ah, now for the hour of the mourning of many, and the pleasant garlands of flowers and the tears, and the moist, dark earth. Ah, for repose down underneath the grass, where the firm feet of the trees grip hold upon the world, where never shall come the wind that now blows through my bones, and the rain shall come warm and trickling, not driven by storm, where is the easeful falling asunder of bone from bone in the dark." Thus prayed Yun-Ilara, who had cursed in his folly and youth, while never heeded Mung.

Still from a heap of bones that are Yun-Ilara still, lying about the ruined base of the tower that once he builded, goes up a shrill voice with the wind crying out for the mercy of Mung, if any such there be.

OF HOW THE GODS WHELMED SIDITH

There was dole in the valley of Sidith. For three years there had been pestilence, and in the last of the three a famine; moreover, there was imminence of war.

Throughout all Sidith men died night and day, and night and day within the Temple of All the gods save One (for none may pray to MANA-YOOD-SUSHAI) did the priests of the gods pray hard.

For they said: "For a long while a man may hear the droning of little insects and yet not be aware that he hath heard them, so may the gods not hear our prayers at first until they have been very oft repeated. But when your praying has troubled the silence long it may be that some god as he strolls in Pegana's glades may come on one of our lost prayers, that flutters like a butterfly tossed in storm when all its wings are broken; then if the gods be merciful they may ease our fears in Sidith, or else they may crush us, being petulant gods, and so we shall see trouble in Sidith no longer, with its pestilence and dearth and fears of war."

But in the fourth year of the pestilence and in the second year of the famine, and while still there was imminence of war, came all the people of Sidith to the door of the Temple of All the gods save One, where none may enter but the priests—but only leave gifts and go.

And there the people cried out: "O High Prophet of All the gods save One, Priest of Kib, Priest of Sish, and Priest of Mung, Teller of the mysteries of Dorozhand, Receiver of the gifts of the People, and Lord of Prayer, what doest thou within the Temple of All the gods save One?"

And Arb-Rin-Hadith, who was the High Prophet, answered: "I pray for all the People."

But the people answered: "O High Prophet of All the gods save One, Priest of Kib, Priest of Sish, and Priest of Mung, Teller of the mysteries of Dorozhand, Receiver of the gifts of the People, and Lord of Prayer, for four long years hast thou prayed with the priests of all thine order, while we brought ye gifts and died. Now, therefore, since They have not heard thee in four grim years, thou must go and carry to Their faces the prayer of the people of Sidith when They go to drive the thunder to his pasture upon the mountain Aghrinaun, or else there shall no longer be gifts upon thy temple door, whenever falls the dew, that thou and thine order may fatten.

"Then thou shalt say before Their faces: 'O All the gods save One, Lords of the Worlds, whose child is the eclipse, take back thy pestilence from Sidith, for ye have played the game of the gods too long with the people of Sidith, who would fain have done with the gods'."

Then in great fear answered the High Prophet, saying: "What if the gods be angry and whelm Sidith?" And the people answered: "Then are we sooner done with pestilence and famine and the imminence of war."

That night the thunder howled upon Aghrinaun, which stood a peak above all others in the land of Sidith. And the people took Arb-Rin-Hadith from his Temple and drave him to Aghrinaun, for they said: "There walk to-night upon the mountain All the gods save One."

And Arb-Rin-Hadith went trembling to the gods.

Next morning, white and frightened from Aghrinaun, came Arb-Rin-Hadith back into the valley, and there spake to the people, saying: "The faces of the gods are iron and their mouths set hard. There is no hope from the gods."

Then said the people: "Thou shalt go to MANA-YOOD-SUSHAI, to whom no man may pray: seek him upon Aghrinaun where it lifts clear into the stillness before morning, and on its summit, where all things seem to rest surely there rests also MANA-YOOD-SUSHAI. Go to him, and say: 'Thou hast made evil gods, and They smite Sidith.' Perchance he hath forgotten all his gods, or hath not heard of Sidith. Thou hast escaped the thunder of the gods, surely thou shalt also escape the stillness of MANA-YOOD-SUSHAI."

Upon a morning when the sky and lakes were clear and the world still, and Aghrinaun was stiller than the world, Arb-Rin-Hadith crept in fear towards the slopes of Aghrinaun because the people were urgent.

All that day men saw him climbing. At night he rested near the top. But ere the morning of the day that followed, such as rose early saw him in the silence, a speck against the blue, stretch up his arms upon the summit to MANA-YOOD-SUSHAI. Then instantly they saw him not, nor was he ever seen of men again who had dared to trouble the stillness of MANA-YOOD-SUSHAI.

Such as now speak of Sidith tell of a fierce and potent tribe that smote away a people in a valley enfeebled by pestilence, where stood a temple to "All the gods save One" in which was no high priest.

OF HOW IMBAUN BECAME HIGH PROPHET IN ARADEC OF ALL THE GODS SAVE ONE

Imbaun was to be made High Prophet in Aradec, of All the Gods save One.

From Ardra, Rhoodra, and the lands beyond came all High Prophets of the Earth to the Temple in Aradec of All the gods save One.

And then they told Imbaun how The Secret of Things was upon the summit of the dome of the Hall of Night, but faintly writ, and in an unknown tongue.

Midway in the night, between the setting and the rising sun, they led Imbaun into the Hall of Night, and said to him, chaunting altogether: "Imbaun, Imbaun, Imbaun, look up to the roof, where is writ The Secret of Things, but faintly, and in an unknown tongue."

And Imbaun looked up, but darkness was so deep within the Hall of Night that Imbaun was not even the High Prophets who came from Ardra, Rhoodra, and the lands beyond, nor saw he aught in the Hall of Night at all.

Then called the High Prophets: "What seest thou, Imbaun?"

And Imbaun said: "I see naught."

Then called the High Prophets: "What knowest thou Imbaun?"

And Imbaun said: "I know naught."

Then spake the High Prophet of Eld of All the gods save One, who is first on Earth of prophets: "O Imbaun! we have all looked upwards in the Hall of Night towards the secret of Things, and ever it was dark, and the Secret faint and in an unknown tongue. And now thou knowest what all High Prophets know."

And Imbaun answered: "I know."

So Imbaun became High Prophet in Aradec of All the gods save One, and prayed for all the people, who knew not that there was darkness in the Hall of Night or that the secret was writ faint and in an unknown tongue.

These are the words of Imbaun that he wrote in a book that all the people might know:

"In the twentieth night of the nine hundredth moon, as night came up the valley, I performed the mystic rites of each of the gods in the temple as is my wont, lest any of the gods should grow angry in the night and whelm us while we slept.

"And as I uttered the last of certain secret words I fell asleep in the temple, for I was weary, with my head against the altar of Dorozhand. Then in the stillness, as I slept, there entered Dorozhand by the temple door in the guise of a man, and touched me on the shoulder, and I awoke.

"But when I saw that his eyes shone blue and lit the whole of the temple I knew that he was a god though he came in mortal guise. And Dorozhand said: 'Prophet of Dorozhand, behold that the people may know.' And he showed me the paths of Sish stretching far down into the future time. Then he bade me arise and follow whither he pointed, speaking no words but commanding with his eyes.

"Therefore upon the twentieth night of the nine hundredth moon I walked with Dorozhand adown the paths of Sish into the future time.

"And ever beside the way did men slay men. And the sum of their slaying was greater than the slaying of the pestilence of any of the evils of the gods.

"And cities arose and shed their houses in dust, and ever the desert returned again to its own, and covered over and hid the last of all that had troubled its repose.

"And still men slew men.

"And I came at last to a time when men set their yoke no longer upon beasts but made them beasts of iron.

"And after that did men slay men with mists.

"Then, because the slaying exceeded their desire, there came peace upon the world that was brought by the hand of the slayer, and men slew men no more.

"And cities multiplied, and overthrew the desert and conquered its repose.

"And suddenly I beheld that THE END was near, for there was a stirring above Pegana as of One who grows weary of resting, and I saw the hound Time crouch to spring, with his eyes upon the throats of the gods, shifting from throat to throat, and the drumming of Skarl grew faint.

"And if a god may fear, it seemed that there was fear upon the face of Dorozhand, and he seized me by the hand and led me back along the paths of Time that I might not see THE END.

"Then I saw cities rise out of the dust again and fall back into the desert whence they had arisen; and again I slept in the Temple of All the gods save One, with my head against the altar of Dorozhand.

"Then again the Temple was alight, but not with light from the eyes of Dorozhand; only dawn came all blue out of the East and shone through the arches of the Temple. Then I awoke and performed the morning rites and mysteries of All the gods save One, lest any of the gods be angry in the day and take away the Sun.

"And I knew that because I who had been so near to it had not beheld THE END that a man should never behold it or know the doom of the gods. This They have hidden."

OF HOW IMBAUN MET ZODRAK

The prophet of the gods lay resting by the river to watch the stream run by.

And as he lay he pondered on the Scheme of Things and the works of all the gods. And it seemed to the prophet of the gods as he watched the stream run by that the Scheme was a right scheme and the gods benignant gods; yet there was sorrow in the Worlds. It seemed that Kib was bountiful, that Mung calmed all who suffer, that Sish dealt not too harshly with the hours, and that all the gods were good; yet there was sorrow in the Worlds.

Then said the prophet of the gods as he watched the stream run by: "There is some other god of whom naught is writ." And suddenly the prophet was aware of an old man who bemoaned beside the river, crying: "Alas! alas!"

His face was marked by the sign and the seal of exceeding many years, and there was yet vigour in his frame. These be the words of the prophet that he wrote in his book: "I said: 'Who art thou that bemoans beside the river?' And he answered: 'I am the fool.' I said: 'Upon thy brow are the marks of wisdom such as is stored in books.' He said: 'I am Zodrak. Thousands of years ago I tended sheep upon a hill that sloped towards the sea. The gods have many moods. Thousands of years ago They were in a mirthful mood. They said: 'Let Us call up a man before Us that We may laugh in Pegāna.'"

"'And Their eyes that looked on me saw not me alone but also saw THE BEGINNING and THE END and all the Worlds besides. Then said the gods, speaking as speak the gods: "Go, back to thy sheep."

"'But I, who am the fool, had heard it said on earth that whoso seeth the gods upon Pegana becometh as the gods, if so he demand to Their faces, who may not slay him who hath looked them in the eyes.

"'And I, the fool, said: "I have looked in the eyes of the gods, and I demand what a man may demand of the gods when he hath seen Them in Pegana." And the gods inclined Their heads and Hoodrazai said: "It is the law of the gods."

"'And I, who was only a shepherd, how could I know?

"'I said: "I will make men rich." And the gods said: "What is rich?"

"'And I said: "I will send them love." And the gods said: "What is love?" And I sent gold into the Worlds, and, alas! I sent with it poverty and strife. And I sent love into the Worlds, and with it grief.

"'And now I have mixed gold and love most woefully together, and I can never remedy what I have done, for the deeds of the gods are done, and nothing may undo them.

"'Then I said: "I will give men wisdom that they may be glad." And those who got my wisdom found that they knew nothing, and from having been happy became glad no more.

"'And I, who would make men happy, have made them sad, and I have spoiled the beautiful scheme of the gods.

"'And now my hand is for ever on the handle of Their plough. I was only a shepherd, and how should I have known?

"'Now I come to thee as thou restest by the river to ask of thee thy forgiveness, for I would fain have the forgiveness of a man.'

"And I answered: 'O Lord of seven skies, whose children are the storms, shall a man forgive a god?'

"He answered: 'Men have sinned not against the gods as the gods have sinned against men since I came into Their councils.'

"And I, the prophet, answered: 'O Lord of seven skies, whose plaything is the thunder, thou art amongst the gods, what need hast thou for words from any man?'

"He said: 'Indeed I am amongst the gods, who speak to me as they speak to other gods, yet is there always a smile about Their mouths, and a look in Their eyes that saith: "Thou wert a man."'

"I said: 'O Lord of seven skies, about whose feet the Worlds are as drifted sand, because thou biddest me, I, a man, forgive thee.'

"And he answered: 'I was but a shepherd, and I could not know.' Then he was gone."

PEGANA

The prophet of the gods cried out to the gods: "O! All the gods save One" for none may pray to MANA-YOOD-SUSHAI, "where shall the life of a man abide when Mung hath made against his body the sign of Mung?—for the people with whom ye play have sought to know."

But the gods answered, speaking through the mist:

"Though thou shouldst tell thy secrets to the beasts, even that the beasts should understand, yet will not the gods divulge the secret of the gods to thee, that gods and beasts and men shall be all the same, all knowing the same things."

That night Yoharneth-Lahai same to Aradec, and said unto Imbaun: "Wherefore wouldst thou know the secret of the gods that not the gods may tell thee?

"When the wind blows not, where, then, is the wind?

"Or when thou art not living, where art thou?

"What should the wind care for the hours of calm or thou for death?

"Thy life is long, Eternity is short.

"So short that, shouldst thou die and Eternity should pass, and after the passing of Eternity thou shouldst live again, thou wouldst say: 'I closed mine eyes but for an instant.'

"There is an eternity behind thee as well as one before. Hast thou bewailed the aeons that passed without thee, who art so much afraid of the aeons that shall pass?"

Then said the prophet: "How shall I tell the people that the gods have not spoken and their prophet doth not know? For then should I be prophet no longer, and another would take the people's gifts instead of me."

Then said Imbaun to the people: "The gods have spoken, saying: 'O Imbaun, Our prophet, it is as the people believe whose wisdom hath discovered the secret of the gods, and the people when they die shall come to Pegana, and there live with the gods, and there have pleasure without toil. And Pegana is a place all white with the peaks of mountains, on each of them a god, and the people shall lie upon the slopes of the mountains each under the god that he hath worshipped most when his lot was in the Worlds. And there shall music beyond thy dreaming come drifting through the scent of all the orchards in the Worlds, with somewhere someone singing an old song that shall be as a half-remembered thing. And there shall be gardens that have always sunlight, and streams that are lost in no sea beneath skies for ever blue. And there shall be no rain nor no regrets. Only the roses that in highest Pegana have achieved their prime shall shed their petals in showers at thy feet, and only far away on the forgotten earth shall voices drift up to thee that cheered thee in thy childhood about the gardens of thy youth. And if thou sighest for any memory of earth because thou hearest unforgotten voices, then will the gods send messengers on wings to soothe thee in Pegana, saying to them: "There one sigheth who hath remembered Earth." And they shall make Pegana more seductive for thee still, and they shall take thee by the hand and whisper in thine ear till the old voices are forgot.

"'And besides the flowers of Pegana there shall have climbed by then until it hath reached to Pegana the rose that clambered about the house where thou wast born. Thither shall also come the wandering echoes of all such music as charmed thee long ago.

"'Moreover, as thou sittest on the orchard lawns that clothe Pegana's mountains, and as thou hearkenest to melody that sways the souls of the gods, there shall stretch away far down beneath thee the great unhappy Earth, till gazing from rapture upon sorrows thou shalt be glad that thou wert dead.

"'And from the three great mountains that stand aloof and over all the others—Grimbol, Zeebol, and Trehagobol—shall blow the wind of the morning and the wind of all the day, borne upon the wings of all the butterflies that have died upon the Worlds, to cool the gods and Pegana.

"'Far through Pegana a silvery fountain, lured upward by the gods from the Central Sea, shall fling its waters aloft, and over the highest of Pegana's peaks, above Trehagobol, shall burst into gleaming mists, to cover Highest Pegana, and make a curtain about the resting-place of MANA-YOOD-SUSHAI.

"'Alone, still and remote below the base of one of the inner mountains, lieth a great blue pool.

"'Whoever looketh down into its waters may behold all his life that was upon the Worlds and all the deeds that he hath done.

"'None walk by the pool and none regard its depths, for all in Pegana have suffered and all have sinned some sin, and it lieth in the pool.

"'And there is no darkness in Pegana, for when night hath conquered the sun and stilled the Worlds and turned the white peaks of Pegana into grey then shine the blue eyes of the gods like sunlight on the sea, where each god sits upon his mountain.

"'And at the Last, upon some afternoon, perhaps in summer, shall the gods say, speaking to the gods: "What is the likeness of MANA-YOOD-SUSHAI and what THE END?"

"'And then shall MANA-YOOD-SUSHAI draw back with his hand the mists that cover his resting, saying: "This is the Face of MANA-YOOD-SUSHAI and this THE END."'"

Then said the people to the prophet: "Shall not black hills draw round in some forsaken land, to make a vale-wide cauldron wherein the molten rock shall seethe and roar, and where the crags of mountains shall be hurled upward to the surface and bubble and go down again, that there our enemies may boil for ever?" And the prophet answered: "It is writ large about the bases of Pegana's mountains, upon which sit the gods: 'Thine Enemies Are Forgiven.'"

THE SAYINGS OF IMBAUN

The Prophet of the gods said: "Yonder beside the road there sitteth a false prophet; and to all who seek to know the hidden days he saith: 'Upon the morrow the King shall speak to thee as his chariot goeth by.'"

Moreover, all the people bring him gifts, and the false prophet hath more to listen to his words than hath the Prophet of the gods.

Then said Imbaun: "What knoweth the Prophet of the gods? I know only that I and men know naught concerning the gods or aught concerning men. Shall I, who am their prophet, tell the people this?

"For wherefore have the people chosen prophets but that they should speak the hopes of the people, and tell the people that their hopes be true?"

The false prophet saith: "Upon the morrow the king shall speak to thee."

Shall not I say: "Upon The Morrow the gods shall speak with thee as thou restest upon Pegana?"

So shall the people be happy, and know that their hopes be true who have believed the words that they have chosen a prophet to say.

But what shall know the Prophet of the gods, to whom none may come to say: "Thy hopes are true," for whom none may make strange signs before his eyes to quench his fear of death, for whom alone the chaunt of his priests availeth naught?

The Prophet of the gods hath sold his happiness for wisdom, and hath given his hopes for the people.

Said also Imbaun: "When thou art angry at night observe how calm be the stars; and shall small ones rail when there is such a calm among the great ones? Or when thou art angry by day regard the distant hills, and see the calm that doth adorn their faces. Shalt thou be angry while they stand so serene?

"Be not angry with men, for they are driven as thou art by Dorozhand. Do bullocks goad one another on whom the same yoke rests?

"And be not angry with Dorozhand, for then thou beatest thy bare fingers against iron cliffs.

"All that is is so because it was to be. Rail not, therefore, against what is, for it was all to be."

And Imbaun said: "The Sun ariseth and maketh a glory about all the things that he seeth, and drop by drop he turneth the common dew to every kind of gem. And he maketh a splendour in the hills.

"And also man is born. And there rests a glory about the gardens of his youth. Both travel afar to do what Dorozhand would have them do.

"Soon now the sun will set, and very softly come twinkling in the stillness all the stars.

"Also man dieth. And quietly about his grave will all the mourners weep.

"Will not his life arise again somewhere in all the worlds? Shall he not again behold the gardens of his youth? Or does he set to end?"

OF HOW IMBAUN SPAKE OF DEATH TO THE KING

There trod such pestilence in Aradec that, the King as he looked abroad out of his palace saw men die. And when the King saw Death he feared that one day even the King should die. Therefore he commanded guards to bring before him the wisest prophet that should be found in Aradec.

Then heralds came to the temple of All the gods save One, and cried aloud, having first commanded silence, crying: "Rhazahan, King over Aradec, Prince by right of Ildun and Ildaun, and Prince by conquest of Pathia, Ezek, and Azhan, Lord of the Hills, to the High Prophet of All the gods save One sends salutations."

Then they bore him before the King.

The King said unto the prophet: "O Prophet of All the gods save One, shall I indeed die?"

And the prophet answered: "O King! thy people may not rejoice for ever, and some day the King will die."

And the King answered: "This may be so, but certainly thou shalt die. It may be that one day I shall die, but till then the lives of the people are in my hands."

Then guards led the prophet away.

And there arose prophets in Aradec who spake not of death to Kings.

OF OOD

Men say that if thou comest to Sundari, beyond all the plains, and shalt climb to his summit before thou art seized by the avalanche which sitteth always on his slopes, that then there lie before thee many peaks. And if thou shalt climb these and cross their valleys (of which there be seven and also seven peaks) thou shalt come at last to the land of forgotten hills, where amid many valleys and white snow there standeth the "Great Temple of One god Only."

Therein is a dreaming prophet who doeth naught, and a drowsy priesthood about him.

These be the priests of MANA-YOOD-SUSHAI.

Within the temple it is forbidden to work, also it is forbidden to pray. Night differeth not from day within its doors. They rest as MANA rests. And the name of their prophet is Ood.

Ood is a greater prophet than any of all the prophets of Earth, and it hath been said by some that were Ood and his priests to pray chaunting all together and calling upon MANA-YOOD-SUSHAI that MANA-YOOD-SUSHAI would then awake, for surely he would hear the prayers of his own prophet—then would there be Worlds no more.

There is also another way to the land of forgotten hills, which is a smooth road and a straight, that lies through the heart of the mountains. But for certain hidden reasons it were better for thee to go by the peaks and snow, even though thou shouldst perish by the way, that thou shouldst seek to come to the house of Ood by the smooth, straight road.

THE RIVER

There arises a river in Pegana that is neither a river of water nor yet a river of fire, and it flows through the skies and the Worlds to the Rim of the Worlds, a river of silence. Through all the Worlds are sounds, the noises of moving, and the echoes of voices and song; but upon the River is no sound ever heard, for there all echoes die.

The River arises out of the drumming of Skarl, and flows for ever between banks of thunder, until it comes to the waste beyond the Worlds, behind the farthest star, down to the Sea of Silence.

I lay in the desert beyond all cities and sounds, and above me flowed the River of Silence through the sky; and on the desert's edge night fought against the Sun, and suddenly conquered.

Then on the River I saw the dream-built ship of the god Yoharneth-Lahai, whose great prow lifted grey into the air above the River of Silence.

Her timbers were olden dreams dreamed long ago, and poets' fancies made her tall, straight masts, and her rigging was wrought out of the people's hopes.

Upon her deck were rowers with dream-made oars, and the rowers were the people of men's fancies, and princes of old story and people who had died, and people who had never been.

These swung forward and swung back to row Yoharneth-Lahai through the Worlds with never a sound of rowing. For ever on every wind float up to Pegana the hopes and the fancies of the people which have no home in the

Worlds, and there Yoharneth-Lahai weaves them into dreams, to take them to the people again.

And every night in his dream-built ship Yoharneth-Lahai setteth forth, with all his dreams on board, to take again their old hopes back to the people and all forgotten fancies.

But ere the day comes back to her own again, and all the conquering armies of the dawn hurl their red lances in the face of the night, Yoharneth-Lahai leaves the sleeping Worlds, and rows back up the River of Silence, that flows from Pegana into the Sea of Silence that lies beyond the Worlds.

And the name of the River is Imrana the River of Silence. All they that be weary of the sound of cities and very tired of clamour creep down in the night-time to Yoharneth-Lahai's ship, and going aboard it, among the dreams and the fancies of old times, lie down upon the deck, and pass from sleeping to the River, while Mung, behind them, makes the sign of Mung because they would have it so. And, lying there upon the deck among their own remembered fancies, and songs that were never sung, and they drift up Imrana ere the dawn, where the sound of the cities comes not, nor the voice of the thunder is heard, nor the midnight howl of Pain as he gnaws at the bodies of men, and far away and forgotten bleat the small sorrows that trouble all the Worlds.

But where the River flows through Pegana's gates, between the great twin constellations Yum and Gothum, where Yum stands sentinel upon the left and Gothum upon the right, there sits Sirami, the lord of All Forgetting. And, when the ship draws near, Sirami looketh with his sapphire eyes into the faces and beyond them of those that were weary of cities, and as he gazes, as one that looketh before him remembering naught, he gently waves his hands. And amid the waving of Sirami's hands there fall from all that behold him all their memories, save certain things that may not be forgotten even beyond the Worlds.

It hath been said that when Skarl ceases to drum, and MANA-YOOD-SUSHAI awakes, and the gods of Pegana know that it is THE END, that then the gods will enter galleons of gold, and with dream-born rowers glide down Imrana (who knows whither or why?) till they come where the River enters the Silent Sea, and shall there be gods of nothing, where nothing is, and never a sound shall come. And far away upon the River's banks shall bay their old hound Time, that shall seek to rend his masters; while MANA-YOOD-SUSHAI shall think some other plan concerning gods and worlds.

THE BIRD OF DOOM AND THE END

For at the last shall the thunder, fleeing to escape from the doom of the gods, roar horribly among the Worlds; and Time, the hound of the gods, shall bay hungrily at his masters because he is lean with age.

And from the innermost of Pegana's vales shall the bird of doom, Mosahn, whose voice is like the trumpet, soar upward with boisterous beatings of his wings above Pegana's mountains and the gods, and there with his trumpet voice acclaim THE END.

Then in the tumult and amid the fury of their hound the gods shall make for the last time in Pegana the sign of all the gods, and go with dignity and quiet down to Their galleons of gold, and sail away down the River of Silence, not ever to return.

Then shall the River overflow its banks, and a tide come setting in from the Silent Sea, till all the Worlds and the Skies are drowned in silence; while MANA-YOOD-SUSHAI in the Middle of All sits deep in thought. And the hound Time, when all the Worlds and cities are swept away whereon he used to raven, having no more to devour, shall suddenly die.

But there are some that hold—and this is the heresy of the Saigoths—that when the gods go down at the last into their galleons of gold Mung shall turn alone, and, setting his back against Trehagobol and wielding the Sword of Severing which is called Death, shall fight out his last fight with the hound Time, his empty scabbard Sleep clattering loose beside him.

There under Trehagobol they shall fight alone when all the gods are gone.

And the Saigoths say that for two days and nights the hound shall leer and snarl before the face of Mung-days and nights that shall be lit by neither sun nor moons, for these shall go dipping down the sky with all the Worlds as the galleons glide away, because the gods that made them are gods no more.

And then shall the hound, springing, tear out the throat of Mung, who, making for the last time the sign of Mung, shall bring down Death crashing through the shoulders of the hound, and in the blood of Time that Sword shall rust away.

Then shall MANA-YOOD-SUSHAI be all alone, with neither Death nor Time, and never the hours singing in his ears, nor the swish of the passing lives.

But far away from Pegana shall go the galleons of gold that bear the gods away, upon whose faces shall be utter calm, because They are the gods knowing that it is THE END.